Bond
No.1 for exam success

Verbal Reasoning

Assessment Papers

Stretch

10–11+ years

OXFORD
UNIVERSITY PRESS

UNIVERSITY PRESS

Great Clarendon Street, Oxford, OX2 6DP, United Kingdom

Oxford University Press is a department of the University of Oxford.
It furthers the University's objective of excellence in research,
scholarship, and education by publishing worldwide. Oxford is
a registered trade mark of Oxford University Press in the UK and in
certain other countries

British Library Cataloguing in Publication Data
Data available

978-0-19-274217-9

10 9

Paper used in the production of this book is a natural, recyclable
product made from wood grown in sustainable forests.
The manufacturing process conforms to the environmental
regulations of the country of origin.

Printed in Poland by Opolgraf SA

Acknowledgements

The publishers would like to thank the following for permissions to
use copyright material:

Page make-up: GreenGate Publishing Services, Tonbridge, Kent
Cover illustrations: Lo Cole

Although we have made every effort to trace and contact all
copyright holders before publication this has not been possible in all
cases. If notified, the publisher will rectify any errors or omissions at
the earliest opportunity.

Links to third party websites are provided by Oxford in good faith
and for information only. Oxford disclaims any responsibility for
the materials contained in any third party website referenced in
this work.

Introduction

What is Bond?

The Bond *Stretch* titles are the most challenging of the Bond Assessment papers, the number one series for the 11+, selective exams and general practice. Bond Stretch is carefully designed to challenge above and beyond the level provided in the regular Bond assessment range.

How does this book work?

The book contains two distinct sets of papers, along with full answers and a Progress Chart:

- Focus tests, accompanied by advice and directions, which are focused on particular (and age-appropriate) Verbal Reasoning question types encountered in the 11+ and other exams, but devised at a higher level than the standard Assessment papers. Each Focus test is designed to help raise a child's skills in the question type as well as offer plenty of practice for the necessary techniques.

- Mixed tests, which are full-length tests containing a full range of Verbal Reasoning question types. These are designed to provide rigorous practice, perhaps against the clock, for children working at a level higher than that required to pass the 11+ and other Verbal Reasoning tests.

- Full answers are provided for both types of test in the middle of the book.

- At the back of the book, there is a Progress Chart which allows you to track your child's progress.

How much time should the tests take?

The tests are for practice and to reinforce learning, and you may wish to test exam techniques and working to a set time limit. We would recommend your child spends 50 minutes to answer the 85 questions in each Mixed paper. You can reduce the suggested time by five minutes to practise working at speed.

Using the Progress Chart

The Progress Chart can be used to track Focus test and Mixed paper results over time to monitor how well your child is doing and identify any repeated problems in tackling the different question types.

Always read this type of question carefully, as most of them will have similar _and_ opposite options.

Underline the pair of words which are the most similar in meaning.

Example   come, go   <u>roams, wanders</u>   fear, fare

More than one set of the answers may apply. Look for the most appropriate.

1	rush, hurry	brighten, dawn	celebrate, perform
2	greed, hunger	number, numeral	below, above
3	cat, mouse	dog, wolf	bear, pig
4	how, why	in, on	by, near
5	hard, tough	rough, smooth	flimsy, rigid
6	aunt, grandchild	niece, father	brother, sister

6

Find the word that is opposite in meaning to the word in capital letters and that rhymes with the second word.

Example   SHARP   front   <u>blunt</u>

7 LOWER   graze   _______________

8 LOVE   wait   _______________

9 POLITE   food   _______________

10 SLOW   flick   _______________

11 IMMENSE   cute   _______________

12 LIE   youth   _______________

If you cannot find a suitable opposite word, try experimenting with rhyming words.

6

Underline the one word in the brackets which will go equally well with each of the words outside the brackets.

Example   word, paragraph, sentence   (pen, cap, <u>letter</u>, top, stop)

13 pillow, blanket, duvet   (night, bed, bedroom, rug)

14 pink, brown, yellow   (crayons, rainbow, paint, grey)

15 Birmingham, Cardiff, Belfast   (England, Leeds, Paris, Europe)

16 oak, ash, willow   (cricket, shrub, beech, country)

17 page, chapter, index   (writer, contents, capital, pencil)

18 traffic, bedside, moon   (car, street, room, light)

○ 6

Underline the two words, one from each group, which are the most opposite in meaning.

Example   (dawn, <u>early</u>, wake)   (<u>late</u>, stop, sunrise)

19 (brave, shy, ask)   (deny, hero, timid)

20 (rise, up, climb)   (high, low, down)

21 (rainy, dry, sunny)   (wet, cloudy, icy)

22 (twin, match, similar)   (opposite, same, alike)

23 (crying, laugh, happy)   (smiling, sad, joy)

24 (find, hide, seek)   (win, lose, loose)

Remember: opposites not similar.

○ 6

Underline the one word in the brackets which will go with the word outside the brackets in the same way as the first two words go together.

Example   good, better   bad, (naughty, worst, <u>worse</u>, nasty)

25 tired, sleepy   awake, (daytime, alert, bed, up)

26 even, odd   level, (flat, peculiar, floor, sloping)

27 mystery, solve   task, (perform, relax, brain, reach)

28 board, cup   cause, (saucer, plank, be, reason)

29 large, vast   jog, (run, crawl, sprint, trot)

30 stripe, strip   peace, (calm, part, take, pace)

Make sure you match the second pair of words in the same way as the first.

○ 6

Now go to the Progress Chart to record your score!   Total ○ 30

 Sorting words

Underline the one word in the brackets which will go equally well with both the pairs of words outside the brackets.

Example   rush, attack   cost, fee   (price, hasten, strike, <u>charge</u>, money)

> Take care. Often each word in the brackets will go well with one lot of words. Look for one that goes well with both.

1 command, control   law, guideline   (measure, rule, govern, call, lead)

2 timepiece, clock   observe, monitor   (time, look, pay attention, regard, watch)

3 cut, trim   slap, smack   (clip, prune, strike, slice, cuff)

4 pale, not dark   gentle, soft   (faint, delicate, flimsy, light, bright)

5 adorable, charming sugary, honeyed   (cute, lovable, sweet, pleasant, fine)

6 movement, flow   modern, present   (push, now, river, current, run)

Find the three-letter word which can be added to the letters in capitals to make a new word. The new word will complete the sentence sensibly.

Example   The cat sprang onto the MO. <u>USE</u>

> For these questions, use the sense of the sentence to help you make a sensible guess.

7 I will RY your books for you if your arm is too sore. _____________

8 You must drink lots of WR every day to stay healthy. _____________

9 The fairy GODMOR helped Cinderella to go to the ball. _____________

10 Pat has lots of goldfish in his GAR pond. _____________

11 Little Monica is too NG to learn to tie her shoelaces. _____________

12 All the cars, lorries and BS drove more slowly in the heavy rain.

____

Rearrange the muddled words in capital letters so that each sentence makes sense.

Example There are sixty SNODCES <u>seconds</u> in a UTMINE <u>minute</u>.

13 Use the BZRAE _____________ crossing to FESLAY _____________ cross the road.

14 The CCIRKTE _____________ match was stopped as it REPODU _____________ with rain.

15 The High ETSRET _____________ shops were full of sale GRABNSAI _____________.

16 The RNHCABSE _____________ of the trees were GNIMVO _____________ in the wind.

17 The train PPESTOD _____________ at the ATSIONT _____________ for a long time.

18 The circus clowns made NEERVOEY _____________ HGULA _____________.

⬤ 6

Underline two words, one from each group, that go together to form a new word. The word in the first group always comes first.

Example (hand, <u>green</u>, for)   (light, <u>house</u>, sure)

19 (in, post, hill)   (stance, stamp, steep)

20 (thin, fat, part)   (nor, her, nets)

21 (up, ape, can)   (pear, start, down)

22 (came, son, high)   (light, down, lives)

23 (an, in, to)   (grey, gather, other)

24 (off, of, on)   (sit, put, ten)

> Take one word at a time from the left bracket and put it in front of each of the right bracket words.

⬤ 6

Find a word that can be put either in front or at the end of each of the following words to make new, compound words.

Example cast   fall   ward   pour   <u>down</u>

25 right   load   roar   stairs   _____________

26 corn   gun   pet   per   _____________

27 stream   bath   shot   thirsty   _____________

28 knock   black   wash   blow   _____________

29 false   brother   child   mother   _____________

30 out   lamp   hole   pipe   _____________

⬤ 6

Focus test 3 Selecting letters

Which one letter can be added to the front of all of these words to make new words?

Experiment with putting various letters in front of each of the words until you hit on the correct one.

Example <u>c</u>are <u>c</u>at <u>c</u>rate <u>c</u>all

1 __ear	__row	__rip	__lad
2 __utter	__read	__east	__ladder
3 __ridge	__ear	__our	__lower
4 __bout	__board	__round	__tone
5 __lever	__able	__oast	__rate

5

Find the letter that will end the first word and start the second word.

Example drow (<u>n</u>) ought

6 ho (__) ater

7 gree (__) ever

8 bette (__) ose

9 danc (__) ver

4

Look at the word on the left and find various letters that could finish that word. Then see which one you can use to start the word on the right.

Find the two letters that will end the first word and start the second word.

Example pas (<u>ta</u>) ste

10 becau (__ __) at

11 ga (__ __) ner

12 traff (__ __) icle

13 chur (__ __) icken

4

Find the letter which will complete both pairs of words, ending the first word and starting the second. The same letter must be used for both pairs of words.

Example mea (<u>t</u>) able   fi (<u>t</u>) ub

14 carro (__) iger   burn (__) ry

15 gre (__) ellow   tr (__) et

16 cur (__) est   or (__) end

17 stic (__) nit   struc (__) ing

Move one letter from the first word and add it to the second word to make two new words.

Example   hunt   sip   <u>hut</u>   <u>snip</u>

18 plane   last   ____________   ____________

19 drift   hear   ____________   ____________

20 treason   seam   ____________   ____________

21 platter   pear   ____________   ____________

22 freight   fed   ____________   ____________

Add one letter to the word in capital letters to make a new word. The meaning of the new word is given in the clue.

Example   PLAN   simple   <u>plain</u>

23 HARD   listened   ____________

24 BITER   sour   ____________

25 SUCK   glued   ____________

26 BOAT   brag   ____________

Remove one letter from the word in capital letters to leave a new word. The meaning of the new word is given in the clue.

Example   AUNT an insect <u>ant</u>

27 PLOTTER   clay worker   ____________

28 DANGER   fury   ____________

29 PRICKLE   chutney   ____________

30 WARY   droll   ____________

Now go to the Progress Chart to record your score!   Total   30

Focus test 4   Finding words

Underline the two words which are the odd ones out in the following groups
of words.

Example   black <u>king</u> purple green <u>house</u>

Three of the words have something in common. Look for the link.
Above, it is colours.

1 suitcase	bag	crayon	ornament	rucksack
2 minute	clock	small	tiny	watch
3 lion	giraffe	bear	leopard	tiger
4 go	stay	leave	remain	depart
5 consider	ponder	think	educate	exercise
6 battle	engine	elephant	bath	brilliance

6

Change the first word of the third pair in the same way as the other pairs to
give a new word.

Example   bind, hind   bare, hare   but, <u>hut</u>

7 climb, limb	plate, late	drain, _________
8 boat, beat	moan, mean	load, _________
9 said, aids	shear, hears	slime, _________
10 card, dark	leap, peak	fool, _________
11 plea, leap	near, earn	mite, _________
12 sold, sale	moth, mate	pony, _________

6

Underline the one word in each group which **cannot be made** from the
letters of the word in capital letters.

Example   STATIONERY   stone   tyres   ration   <u>nation</u>   noisy

13 CHARACTER	tracer	carer	chart	church	cheat
14 BREAKING	baking	grain	banker	brink	engine
15 PLASTERER	plates	treats	please	pester	repast

3

Underline the one word in each group which **can be made** from the letters of the word in capital letters.

Example CHAMPION   camping   notch   peach   cramp   <u>chimp</u>

16 WANDERING   dangers   dawning   raining   drawer   window

17 DRAGONFLY   lagoon   grandly   found   larder   fondle

18 TROMBONE   noble   broth   number   broom   tremor

Underline the two words in each line which are made from the same letters.

Example TAP   PET   <u>TEA</u>   POT   <u>EAT</u>

19 DUSTY   DIRTY   RADIO   RODEO   STUDY

20 BLASTS   STABLE   BLADES   BLEATS   LABELS

21 TOWELS   STROLL   LOWEST   SWELLS   TEASEL

22 PRICES   PRINCE   PRIEST   CENTRE   STRIPE

23 STORES   SOREST   TRUSTS   STROKE   STRAIT

24 TREATS   LEARNT   STEERS   TRAILS   ANTLER

Find the four-letter word hidden in each sentence. Each begins at the end of one word and ends at the beginning of another word, and can cover two or three words. The order of the letters may not be changed.

Example We had ba<u>ts and</u> balls.   <u>sand</u>

25 I saw her as I was walking down the road. ______________

26 As I am tall, I can reach every book on the shelf. ______________

27 Today the weather is cold for the time of year. ______________

28 Mudit's hands were cold as he had forgotten his gloves. ______________

29 Do not forget that the mayor is coming to school tomorrow.

____

30 Mondays are my worst days of the week in term time. ______________

Look at the first group of three words. The word in the middle has been made from the two other words. Complete the second group of three words in the same way, making a new word in the middle.

Example   PA<u>IN</u>   INTO   T<u>OO</u>K   ALSO   <u>SOON</u>   ONLY

> Look carefully at the first set of three words. Sometimes the pattern is straightforward, as in these:

1 CARE   RENT   WANT   FIRE   ____________   MOST
2 PAID   PATH   THIN   STEM   ____________   OPAL
3 BARE   CARE   COMB   TIME   ____________   MAUL
4 ICED   WISH   WASH   OPEN   ____________   BATH
5 LIFE   TAIL   ATOM   DISH   ____________   ARCH

> Sometimes, letters have to be worked out individually or there are several options with repeat letters:

6 PAIN   PANE   ENDS   CROP   ____________   WORK
7 BALL   BABY   BUOY   TIME   ____________   SUNS
8 DRAW   WIND   WINK   MUFF   ____________   GROW
9 POLE   LATE   TALL   KIND   ____________   RACE
10 BOAT   COMB   COME   KNIT   ____________   PEAR
11 TREE   BEAT   BOAT   EVIL   ____________   MUCH
12 BOAT   ATOM   MATE   FATE   ____________   RUSK
13 TOAD   COAT   ACTS   TINY   ____________   SPIN
14 EACH   AREA   ARCH   ANTS   ____________   BEAK
15 LEAF   FOIL   LION   LASH   ____________   DRUM

5

10

Change the first word into the last word, by changing one letter at a time and making a new, different word in the middle.

Example	CASE	<u>CASH</u>	LASH
16	CRAB	_____________	GRUB
17	PRIM	_____________	PRAY
18	SAKE	_____________	BIKE
19	CAGE	_____________	BAKE
20	FIRM	_____________	TIRE

5

Change the first word into the last word, by changing one letter at a time and making two new, different words in the middle.

Example	CASE	<u>CASH</u>	<u>WASH</u>	WISH
21	WICK	_____________	_____________	SUCH
22	ROAD	_____________	_____________	LARD
23	WIDE	_____________	_____________	FIRM
24	SOFT	_____________	_____________	LOUD
25	BOOK	_____________	_____________	LUCK
26	TALL	_____________	_____________	TOAD
27	DRIP	_____________	_____________	TRAY
28	COOL	_____________	_____________	FOUR
29	LANE	_____________	_____________	FIND
30	FULL	_____________	_____________	FAIR

10

Now go to the Progress Chart to record your score! Total **30**

If A = 6, B = 3, C = 11, D = 5 and E = 2, what are the values of these calculations? Write each answer as a number.

Replace the letters with numbers and work out the calculations.

1 C − (A + B) = _____

2 D^2 − C = _____

3 EA ÷ B = _____

4 (D + E + A) − C = _____

5 $\dfrac{(C + D)}{E}$ = _____

5

Using the same values, what are the values of these calculations? Write each answer as a letter.

6 (A + C) − DB = _____

7 (C + D) − DE = _____

Do exactly the same but turn the number answer into its letter value.

2

If T = 4, B = 7, R = 3, A = 1, D = 5 and O = 2, find the sum of these words when the letters are added together.

8 BOAT _____   **9** TOAD _____   **10** ROOT _____

3

Read the first two statements and then underline one of the four options below that must be true.

More than one statement may be true, but you must look for the only one that has to be true, given the information.

11 'Maya loves going on holiday. This year she is going to Greece.'

   A Last year Maya went to France.

   B Maya likes Greece best.

   C Maya is going to Greece.

   D Greece is a popular place to go on holiday.

12 'Beetles are a type of insect. Insects have six legs.'

   A All animals are insects.

   B Beetles are small.

   C Animals have six legs.

   D Beetles have six legs.

2

In a test at school out of a total of 40 marks, Jo got half of them right. Kate got only 14 out of 40, while Tina only made seven mistakes. Anya made 11 mistakes and Dhruv got five more right than Jo.

13 Who got the most marks? ________________

14 Who got less than Dhruv but more than Kate? ________________

15 Who got 4 more marks than Dhruv? ________________

○ 3

In French, Adrian sat somewhere to the left of Jasmine who sat somewhere to the left of Robert. Saskia and Jasmine did not sit next to each other. Connor sat next to Mo but not Robert. Mo sat somewhere to the right of Jasmine.

1	2	3	Robert	4	5

LEFT   RIGHT

Where did each child sit?

16 Adrian ______   **17** Jasmine ______   **18** Saskia ______

19 Connor ______   **20** Mo ______

○ 5

SWANSEA   SPALDING   SOUTHAMPTON   SOLIHULL   STOCKPORT
If these towns are put into alphabetical order, which comes:

21 first? _________   **22** last? _________   **23** fourth? _________

○ 3

If the days of the week are put into alphabetical order, which comes:

24 first? _______________   **25** last? _______________

26 the one before Saturday? _______________

27 in the middle? _______________

○ 4

If the letters of the word BREAKING are written alphabetically, which comes:

28 first? ______   **29** fourth? ______   **30** seventh? ______

○ 3

Now go to the Progress Chart to record your score!   Total ○ 30

If the code for GRATEFUL is 5 8 7 3 9 2 1 6.
Encode each of these words using the same codes.

> First line up the
> code with the word:
> G R A T E F U L
> 5 8 7 3 9 2 1 6
> Then substitute the
> letters for numbers.

   1 GATE _____________   **2** FURL _____________

Decode these words using the same code as above.

   3 3 9 7 8 _______________   **4** 3 8 1 9 _______________

5 If the code for SHEPHERD is K T O N T O Z L, what is the code for DRESS? _____________

6 Using the same code, what does K N O O L stand for? _____________

7 If the code for TOMORROW is ↑ ← → ← ↓ ↓ ← ↙, what is the code for WORM? _____________

8 Using the same code, what does ↓ ← ← ↑ stand for? _____________

9 If the code for FOUNTAIN is c X 9 P 8 e @ P, what does P X 9 P stand for? _____________

10 Using the same code, what is the code for INTO? _____________ **10**

Match the right word to each code given below.

       REED   BARE   BEAR   BARB

11 X V W Z _______________

12 X W Z X _______________

13 Z V V Y _______________

14 X W Z V _______________

> Look for some letters that
> stand out. In this case, all the
> words begin with B except one
> and REED also has double E.

15 Using the same code, what does z v w y stand for? _____________ **5**

Solve the problems by working out the letter code. The alphabet has been written out the help you.

A B C D E F G H I J K L M N O P Q R S T U V W X Y Z

Example If the code for CAT is D B U, what is the code for DOG? <u>E P H</u>

16 If the code for TABLE is V C D N G, what is the code for CHAIR?

____

17 If the code for PAPER is Q B Q F S, what does C P P L T mean?

____

18 If the code for HEDGE is F C B E C, what is the code for TREES? _______________

19 If the code for SHELF is O D A H B, what does C N E H H mean? _______________

4

Example If the code for CAB is 3 1 2, what is the code for EGG? <u>5 7 7</u>

20 If the code for DEAF is 4 5 1 6, what is the code for HIGH? _______________

21 If the code for CHAFF is 3 8 1 6 6, what does 1 2 9 4 5 stand for? _______________

2

Example If the code for PEACH is O F Z D G, what is the code for APPLE? <u>Z Q O M D</u>

22 If the code for DRESS is E Q F R T, what is the code for SHIRT? _______________

23 If the code for TREBLE is V Q G A N D, what is the code for VOICE? _______________

24 If the code for STYLE is Q U W M C, what does T P E V C stand for? _______________

25 If the code for MATHS is N B S G T, what does U J L D T stand for? _______________

26 If the code for TIGER is U H H D S, what is the code for ZEBRA? _______________

27 If the code for LAUGH is J Y S E F, what does F Y N N W stand for? _______________

28 If the code for SORRY is R Q Q T X, what is the code for TEARS? _______________

29 If the code for WATER is A Z X D V, what does Z Z P T I stand for? _______________

30 If the code for DIVE is C G S A, what is the code for BEAD? _______________

9

Focus test 8   Sequences

Complete the following sentences in the best way by underlining one word from each set of brackets.

Example   Tall is to (tree, <u>short</u>, colour) as narrow is to (thin, white, <u>wide</u>).

> Look for the relationship between the pairs of statements. The second pairing must be completed in the same way.

1 Snow is to (white, flake, cold) as sun is to (day, world, hot).

2 Dog is to (bark, pet, bone) as (person, cat, mouth) is to speak.

3 Diamond is to (necklace, heart, jewel) as (giant, spade, sports) is to club.

4 (Owl, Other, Clever) is to wise as dense is to (think, thin, thick).

Find the missing letters. The alphabet has been written out to help you.

A B C D E F G H I J K L M N O P Q R S T U V W X Y Z

> Do these in the same way. Look for the pattern. Use the alphabet line to help you.

Example   AB is to CD as PQ is to <u>RS</u>.

5 FG is to JK as PQ is to _____.

6 ZY is to YX as ON is to _____.

7 MK is to IG as EC is to _____.

8 AP is to BQ as CR is to _____.

9 HL is to JJ as RV is to _____.

10 Ta is to Ya as Za is to _____.

11 AZ is to BY as CX is to _____.

12 UN is to WP as YR is to _____.

> Most of the time in these sequences, the letters work independently, like these.

Find the two missing pairs of letters in the following sequences. The alphabet has been written out to help you.

A B C D E F G H I J K L M N O P Q R S T U V W X Y Z

Example   CQ   DP   EQ   FP   GQ   HP

There are two ways of tackling these sequences. Check to see if the letters are working together (as below) or independently as on the previous page.

13 AB   DE   GH   JK   ____   ____

14 ____   XW   VU   TS   ____   PO

15 RS   VW   ____   DE   ____   LM

16 JH   FD   ____   ____   TR   PN

17 MA   NC   ME   ____   MI   ____

18 GV   ____   CV   AW   ____   WW

19 AK   DI   GG   JE   ____   ____

20 ____   XG   VH   ____   RJ   PK

21 CHu   Plv   CJw   ____   ____   PMz

Look at the letters separately with these ones.

Find the two missing numbers in the following sequences.

Example   2 4 6 8 10 12

22 23 25 __ 29 __ 33

23 16 __ 10 __ 4 1

24 __ 30 25 20 15 __

25 2 __ 8 __ 32 64

26 18 17 15 12 __ __

27 __ __ 19 22 24 25

28 20 __ 25 9 30 6 __ 3

29 6 4 6 6 __ __ 6 10

30 17 __ 14 9 __ 10 8 11

Look for the pattern between the numbers.

Sometimes, in these questions, the increase/decrease is irregular.

Check for numbers going up and down. If this is the case, look at alternate numbers.

Mixed paper 1

Underline the pair of words which are the most similar in meaning.

Example   come, go   <u>roams, wanders</u>   fear, fare

  1 top, bottom   glide, soar   leaf, fruit

  2 prick, pierce   needle, thread   sew, mend

  3 combine, alter   crowd, throng   run, hide

  4 pick, mix   stir, sleep   select, choose

  5 fix, break   needy, rich   poor, unfortunate   **5**

Find the three-letter word which can be added to the letters in capitals to make a new word. The new word will complete the sentence sensibly.

Example   The cat sprang onto the MO. <u>USE</u>

  6 Dad put the tools back into the garden D. _______________

  7 "Ready, SDY, go!" shouted the starter at Sports Day. _______________

  8 The puddles were so deep, I got my socks and SS wet.

    ____

  9 I felt guilty because I GOT my friend's birthday. _______________

 10 We studied the Tudors in TORY lessons. _______________   **5**

Which one letter can be added to the front of all of these words to make new words?

Example   <u>c</u>are   <u>c</u>at   <u>c</u>rate   <u>c</u>all

 11 __pine   __hut   __lit   __will

 12 __lag   __arming   __light   __ill

 13 __ear   __hinge   __rite   __on

 14 __at   __aster   __we   __vent

 15 __ink   __otter   __eel   __udder   **5**

Underline the two words which are the odd ones out in the following groups of words.

Example black	<u>king</u>	purple	green	<u>house</u>
16 stone	rock	chalk	hill	mountain
17 basin	tap	bath	map	sink
18 right	left	wrong	correct	accurate
19 under	beneath	below	on	inside
20 Mediterranean	Atlantic	Pacific	Indian	North

5

Look at the first group of three words. The word in the middle has been made from the two other words. Complete the second group of three words in the same way, making a new word in the middle.

Example PA<u>IN</u> INTO <u>T</u>OOK   ALSO   <u>SOON</u>   ONLY

21 JUMP	JUST	MOST	DOOR	______________	PIGS
22 BRIM	BITE	FATE	SLIP	______________	GONG
23 COIN	INTO	TOMB	BAKE	______________	EPIC
24 ZIPS	SPIN	CORN	BINS	______________	JEEP
25 STUD	DUST	STOP	GLUM	______________	USED

5

If a = 4, b = 2, c = 7, d = 3 and e = 5, work out the values of these calculations.

26 $(a + b + c) - (d + e)$ = ____

27 $ae - b$ = ____

28 $(e + c) \div a$ = ____

29 $d^2 - b^2$ = ____

30 $(c - a) + (d - b)$ = ____

5

If the code for SHOPPING is 7 6 1 3 3 5 2 4, what are the codes for the following words?

31 PINS ______________   **33** GOSSIP ______________

32 SING ______________

3

Using the same code, what do the following codes stand for?

34 6 1 3 5 2 4 ______________   **35** 6 5 4 6 ______________

2

Complete the following sentences in the best way by choosing one word from each set of brackets.

Example Tall is to (tree, <u>short</u>, colour) as narrow is to (thin, white, <u>wide</u>).

36 Window is to (glass, view, curtain) as (tree, door, fire) is to wood.

37 Hill is to (mountain, high, cold) as valley is to (river, low, steep).

38 Foal is to (horse, young, race) as lamb is to (kebab, sheep, field).

39 Kettle is to (kitchen, boil, water) as (hot, wash, bath) is to bathroom.

40 (Toe, Shin, Foot) is to leg as finger is to (hand, arm, nail).

Add one letter to the word in capital letters to make a new word. The meaning of the new word is given in the clue.

Example PLAN   simple   <u>plain</u>

41 RIGHT   a scare   ______________

42 SPOT   game   ______________

43 BEAR   facial hair ______________

44 PEAT   fold   ______________

45 CAVE   cut, slice   ______________

Underline two words, one from each group, that go together to form a new word. The word in the first group always comes first.

Example (hand, <u>green</u>, for)   (light, <u>house</u>, sure)

46 (cub, surf, live)   (bend, board, belt)

47 (white, water, green)   (home, proof, cloud)

48 (back, from, sum)   (wood, were, ward)

49 (be, in, on)   (gun, end, sett)

50 (cap, free, card)   (land, oil, able)

Change the first word into the last word, by changing one letter at a time and making a new, different word in the middle.

Example CASE   <u>CASH</u>   LASH

51 FARM   ______________   HARK

52 SNUB   _____________   SNAG

53 LIKE   _____________   WIFE

54 SNOW   _____________   GLOW

55 MANE   _____________   MUTE

In a sports shop, different types of balls were placed in a row of containers. From the information, work out where each type of balls were.

A	B	TABLE TENNIS	C	D	E

The tennis balls were at one end of the display.

The rugby balls and hockey balls were next to each other.

The cricket balls were next to the table tennis balls and the hockey balls.

The footballs were in the spare place.

56 A = _______________   59 D = _______________

57 B = _______________   60 E = _______________

58 C = _______________

Find the word that is opposite in meaning to the word in capital letters and that rhymes with the second word.

Example SHARP   front   <u>blunt</u>

61 CLEAR   paint   _______________

62 KIND   stool   _______________

63 SANE   glad   _______________

64 TIMID   slave   _______________

65 ADORE   wait   _______________

Find the letter that will end the first word and start the second word.

Example drow (<u>n</u>) ought

66 dat (__) very   69 spil (__) iver

67 jaz (__) ebra   70 stuf (__) rog

68 brea (__) ite

Underline the one word in each group which **cannot be made** from the letters of the word in capital letters.

Example STATIONERY   stone   tyres   ration   <u>nation</u>   noisy

71 DISTANCE   stand   dance   stain   caned   nasty

72 STARVING   grand   grants   strain   saving   string

73 SQUEALED   sealed   duels   ladles   deals   eased

74 TRUNCHEON   trench   torch   chant   tenor   thorn

75 SPURTING   spurn   trump   grins   spring   grunts

5

If the code for GARDEN is * @ ? # $ ~, what do the following codes stand for?

76 # ? @ *   ___________

79 * ? $ $ ~   ___________

77 ? @ ~ *   ___________

80 * ? @ # $ ___________

78 ~ $ @ ?   ___________

5

Find the two missing numbers in the following sequences.

Example 2 4 6 8 <u>10</u> <u>12</u>

81 7 17 __ 37 __ 57

82 __ __ 8 16 32 64

83 33 __ 27 24 21 __

84 3 4 6 __ 13 __

85 40 32 __ 19 __ 10

5

Now go to the Progress Chart to record your score!   Total   **85**

Mixed paper 2

Find the two letters that will end the first word and start the second word.

Example pas (<u>ta</u>) ste

1 befo (__ __) ason

4 lem (__ __) ly

2 clo (__ __) ere

5 prin (__ __) iling

3 oli (__ __) st

5

If the code for HEALTHY is ? & * % ^ ? ! what do the following codes stand for?

6 ? & * ^ _______________   **8** % * ^ & % ! _______________

7 ^ * % % _______________

Using the same code, what are the codes for the following words?

9 ALLY _______________   **10** TEETH _______________

Underline the one word in the brackets which will go equally well with each of the words outside the brackets.

Example   word, paragraph, sentence   (pen, cap, <u>letter</u>, top, stop)

11 sun, rain, cloud   (water, weather, shine, dawn, grey)

12 Toyota, Ford, Vauxhall   (car, bike, train, country, garage)

13 lamb, pork, beef   (sheep, field, shop, chicks, meat)

14 heel, toe, ankle   (finger, knuckle, joint, foot, elbow)

15 lily, cannon, ice   (cube, flower, water, ball, gun)

Find the missing letters. The alphabet has been written out to help you.

A B C D E F G H I J K L M N O P Q R S T U V W X Y Z

Example   AB is to CD as PQ is to <u>RS</u>.

16 GH is to KL as OP is to ______.   **19** AQ is to BR as CS is to ______.

17 NL is to JH as FD is to ______.   **20** EC is to DB as CA is to ______.

18 EV is to GT as DW is to ______.

Match these words to the codes below:

FEET   FATE   FINE   NEAT   NINE

21 ❻❾❻⑩ _______________   **24** ❺⑩⑩❹ _______________

22 ❺❾❻⑩ _______________   **25** ❺❸❹⑩ _______________

23 ❻⑩❸❹ _______________

Fill in the crosswords so that all the given words are included. You have been given one or two letters as a clue in each crossword.

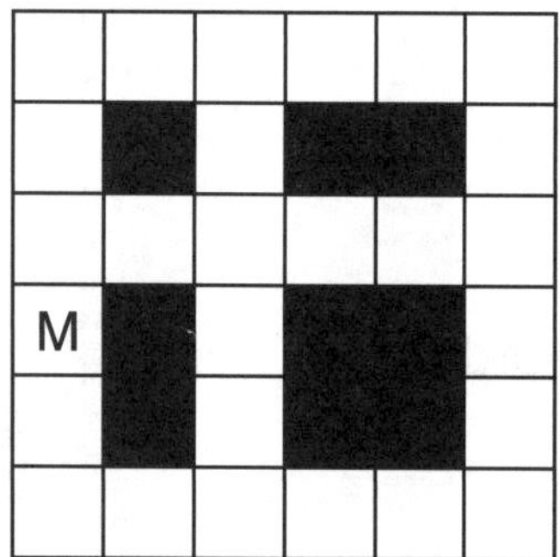

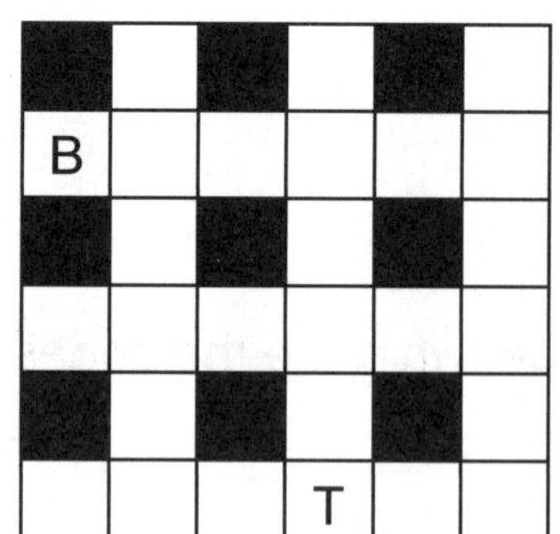

ROLLER RATHER RAREST
FATHER FARMER THRILL

CRATER BUTTER ATTEND
MUTTER STREET TRADER

If the code for FLUTTER is a v y h h o p, what do the following codes stand for?

28 h p y o ______________

30 v o h h o p ______________

29 a v y a a ______________

Remove one letter from the word in capital letters to leave a new word. The meaning of the new word is given in the clue.

Example   AUNT   an insect   <u>ant</u>

31 BLAST   final   ______________

32 SPRING   stem   ______________

33 GRAIN   obtain   ______________

34 BLEAKER   cup   ______________

35 PAINTS   aches   ______________

Underline the two words, one from each group, which are the most opposite in meaning.

Example   (dawn, <u>early</u>, wake)   (<u>late,</u> stop, sunrise)

36 (dim, clever, torn)   (tattered, bright, folded)

37 (mild, cruel, beat)   (harsh, weak, thrash)

38 (better, wicked, rough)   (ready, good, smother)

39 (naught, icy, heat)   (zero, cool, warm)

40 (ours, mine, hole)   (dig, complete, theirs)

2

3

5

5

Find the two missing numbers in the following sequences.

Example 2 4 6 8 <u>10</u> <u>12</u>

41 3 6 12 __ __ 96

44 18 3 18 5 __ __

42 1 3 __ 7 9 __

45 6 4 __ 3 8 __

43 66 __ 44 33 __ 11

Rearrange the muddled words in capital letters so that each sentence makes sense.

Example There are sixty SNODCES <u>seconds</u> in a UTMINE <u>minute</u>.

46 Why can't you SECLO ______________ the door YLTUQIE ______________ ?

47 My REMTOH ______________ went to the KTEMASPREUR ______________ after dropping us at school.

48 In the DSYAHLOI ______________, Petra NDEJIO ______________ a swimming club.

49 The RATIN ______________ stopped at many NSATTIOS ______________ before we reached London.

50 After KRAEB ______________, we have double YRHSOTI ______________.

Underline two words, one from each group, that go together to form a new word. The word in the first group always comes first.

Example (hand, <u>green</u>, for)   (light, <u>house</u>, sure)

51 (plate, cup, chair)   (hair, form, board)

52 (good, bad, by)   (bye, by, buy)

53 (sail, law, fry)   (or, day, year)

54 (were, there, three)   (four, for, fore)

55 (for, in, out)   (cyst, cars, cast)

Underline the one word in each group which **can be made** from the letters of the word in capital letters.

Example CHAMPION   camping   notch   peach   cramp   <u>chimp</u>

56 CARDINAL   larder   danger   cranial   cradle   crayon

57 PREJUDICE   priced   justice   prelude   juicier   erudite

58 PARTICULAR	article	carpal	claret	particle	plural
59 GREATNESS	secret	nastier	agrees	stains	treats
60 YESTERDAY	sturdy	Saturday	strays	starry	trades

Look at the first group of three words. The word in the middle has been made from the two other words. Complete the second group of three words in the same way, making a new word in the middle.

Example PAIN	INTO	T<u>OO</u>K	ALSO	<u>SOON</u>	ONLY
61 KERB	BRAN	NAPE	SOUP	_____________	AMID
62 TALK	LATE	LOBE	LEFT	_____________	NAIL
63 BONE	BEST	DUST	CURL	_____________	BLUE
64 MIST	FIST	FISH	BEAM	_____________	CALF
65 LIVE	LOVE	VOLE	ZOOM	_____________	LIME

Read the first two statements and then underline one of the four options below that must be true.

66 'Not all trees have green leaves. The ash tree has green leaves.'

   A Leaves fall from the trees in winter.

   B Many trees have green leaves.

   C Beech trees may have copper leaves.

   D Ash trees may have many leaves.

67 'Animals are either tame or wild. If animals are scared, they may bite.'

   A Wild animals always bite.

   B Tame animals never bite.

   C Wild animals may bite.

   D Wild animals are scared.

68 If the seasons are put in alphabetical order, which season comes after summer? _____________

69 Write the letters of the word COMPARE in alphabetical order.

____

70 Using the answer for question 69 above, which is now the middle letter? _____

3

Change the first word into the last word, by changing one letter at a time and making a new, different word in the middle.

Example CASE <u>CASH</u> LASH

71 KING _____________ FIND

72 SPOT _____________ HOOT

73 PURR _____________ CURE

74 SIFT _____________ LIFE

75 CORK _____________ COLD

5

If T = 3, L = 6, R = 5, B = 2, E = 1 and A = 4, find the sum of these words when the letters are added together.

76 TABLE _____ **77** LABEL _____ **78** RABBLE _____

79 Using the same code, if the total of BLADDER is 34, work out the value of D. _____

80 Using the same code, if the total of TRAILER is 31, work out the value of I. _____

5

Underline the two words in each line which are made from the same letters.

Example TAP PET <u>TEA</u> POT <u>EAT</u>

81 ASLEEP PLATER TAILOR LAPSES PLEASE

82 TESTER TASTER STREET STEERS ASTERS

83 SNAILS SPINAL PLAINS PALEST STABLE

84 BITERS STRIPE PRISES SPORES TRIBES

85 BLEEPS CHAPEL PEBBLE PLEACH BLEACH

5

Mixed paper 3

Underline the one word in the brackets which will go with the word outside the brackets in the same way as the first two words go together.

Example good, better   bad, (naughty, worst, <u>worse</u>, nasty)

1 apple, pip   plum, (seed, stone, weed, tree)

2 quick, slow   flat, (house, fast, bumpy, room)

3 dog, kennel   cow, (barn, grass, milk, house)

4 bite, tooth   hold, (have, tongue, hand, nail)

5 six, three   four, (legs, five, eight, two)

If $p = 6$, $q = 3$, $r = 2$, $s = 5$, $t = 4$ and $u = 12$, work out the values of these calculations. Write each answer as a letter.

6 $pq - qr$ = _____   9 $p^2 \div q$ = _____

7 $(s + t) - p$ = _____   10 $tp - st$ = _____

8 $(u \div t) + (s - r)$ = _____

Match these codes to the words below.

a y i u   u i a a   a o u i   u o a y

11 STEM   _____________   13 SAME   _____________

12 MAST   _____________   14 MESS   _____________

15 Using the same code, what does y i o u stand for? _______________

Find the four-letter word which can be added to the letters in capitals to make a new word. The new word will complete the sentence sensibly.

Example They enjoyed the BCAST. <u>ROAD</u>

16 Mrs Blunt took her shopping ET and went off to the shops.

____

17 The little mouse SERED quickly back to its hole. _______________

18 That coat is not yours; it BES to Yumi. _______________

19 Mr Brown is angry as he is having trouble TING his car.

____

20 On her birthday, Dad gave Mum a huge bunch of ERS. _______________

Find the letter which will complete both pairs of words, ending the first word and starting the second. The same letter must be used for both pairs of words.

Focus test 1

1 rush, hurry
2 number, numeral
3 dog, wolf
4 by, near
5 hard, tough
6 brother, sister
7 raise
8 hate
9 rude
10 quick
11 minute
12 truth
13 bed
14 grey
15 Leeds
16 beech
17 contents
18 light
19 brave   timid
20 up   down
21 dry   wet
22 similar   opposite
23 happy   sad
24 find   lose
25 alert
26 sloping
27 perform
28 be
29 sprint
30 pace

Focus test 2

1 rule
2 watch
3 clip
4 light
5 sweet
6 current
7 CAR
8 ATE
9 THE
10 DEN
11 YOU
12 USE
13 zebra   safely
14 cricket   poured
15 street   bargains
16 branches   moving
17 stopped   station
18 everyone   laugh
19 instance
20 father
21 upstart
22 highlight
23 another
24 often
25 up
26 pop
27 blood
28 out
29 hood
30 blow

Focus test 3

1 g
2 b
3 f
4 a
5 c
6 w
7 n
8 r
9 e
10 se
11 in
12 ic
13 ch
14 t
15 y
16 b
17 k
18 plan   least
19 rift   heard
20 reason   steam
21 patter   pearl
22 fright   feed
23 heard
24 bitter
25 stuck
26 boast
27 potter
28 anger
29 pickle
30 wry

Focus test 4

1 crayon   ornament
2 clock   watch
3 giraffe   bear
4 stay   remain
5 educate   exercise
6 engine   elephant
7 rain
8 lead
9 limes
10 look
11 item
12 pane
13 church
14 engine
15 treats
16 dawning
17 grandly
18 broom
19 DUSTY   STUDY
20 STABLE   BLEATS
21 TOWELS   LOWEST
22 PRIEST   STRIPE
23 STORES   SOREST
24 LEARNT   ANTLER
25 hero
26 ache
27 fort
28 dash
29 them
30 soft

Focus test 5

1 REST
2 STOP
3 MIME
4 BOTH
5 RAID
6 CROW
7 SITS
8 FROM
9 CARD
10 PEAK
11 MICE
12 TEAR
13 PINT
14 BEAN
15 HURL
16 GRAB
17 PRAM
18 BAKE
19 CAKE
20 FIRE
21 SICK   SUCK
22 LOAD   LORD
23 WIRE   FIRE
24 LOFT   LOUT
25 LOOK   LOCK
26 TOLL   TOLD
27 TRIP   TRAP
28 FOOL   FOUL
29 LINE   FINE
30 FALL   FAIL

Focus test 6

1 2
2 14
3 4
4 2
5 8
6 E
7 A
8 14
9 12
10 11
11 C
12 D
13 Tina
14 Jo
15 Anya
16 2
17 3
18 1
19 5
20 4
21 SOLIHULL
22 SWANSEA
23 STOCKPORT
24 FRIDAY
25 WEDNESDAY
26 MONDAY
27 SUNDAY
28 A
29 G
30 N

Focus test 7

1 5 7 3 9
2 2 1 8 6
3 TEAR
4 TRUE
5 L Z O K K
6 SPEED
7 ↙ ← ↓ →
8 ROOT
9 NOUN
10 @ P 8 X
11 BEAR
12 BARB
13 REED
14 BARE
15 READ
16 E J C K T
17 BOOKS
18 R P C C Q
19 GRILL
20 8978
21 ABIDE
22 T G J Q U
23 X N K B G
24 VOGUE
25 TIMES
26 A D C Q B
27 HAPPY
28 S G Z T R
29 VALUE
30 A C X Z

Focus test 8

1 cold   hot
2 bark   person
3 heart   spade
4 clever   thick
5 TU
6 NM
7 AY
8 DS
9 TT
10 Ea
11 DW
12 AT
13 MN   PQ
14 ZY   RQ

15	ZA	HI
16	BZ	XV
17	NG	NK
18	EW	YV
19	MC	PA
20	ZF	TI
21	PKx	CLy
22	27	31
23	13	7
24	35	10
25	4	16
26	8	3
27	10	15
28	12	35
29	6	8
30	8	11

Mixed paper 1

1 glide, soar
2 prick, pierce
3 crowd, throng
4 select, choose
5 poor, unfortunate
6 SHE
7 TEA
8 HOE
9 FOR
10 HIS
11 s
12 f
13 w
14 e
15 r
16 hill, mountain
17 tap, map
18 left, wrong
19 on, inside
20 Mediterranean, North
21 DOGS
22 SING
23 KEEP
24 SNIP
25 MUGS
26 5
27 18
28 3
29 5
30 4
31 3 5 2 7
32 7 5 2 4
33 4 1 7 7 5 3
34 HOPING
35 HIGH
36 glass, door
37 high, low
38 horse, sheep
39 kitchen, bath
40 toe, arm
41 fright
42 sport
43 beard

44 pleat
45 carve
46 surfboard
47 waterproof
48 backward
49 begun
50 capable
51 HARM
52 SNUG
53 LIFE
54 SLOW
55 MATE
56 tennis balls
57 footballs
58 cricket balls
59 hockey balls
60 rugby balls
61 faint
62 cruel
63 mad
64 brave
65 hate
66 e
67 z
68 k
69 l
70 f
71 nasty
72 grand
73 ladles
74 chant
75 trump
76 DRAG
77 RANG
78 NEAR
79 GREEN
80 GRADE

81	27	47
82	2	4
83	30	18
84	9	18
85	25	14

Mixed paper 2

1 re
2 th
3 ve
4 on
5 ce
6 HEAT
7 TALL
8 LATELY
9 * % % !
10 ^ & & ^ ?
11 weather
12 car
13 meat
14 foot
15 water
16 ST
17 BZ

18 FU
19 DT
20 BZ
21 NINE
22 FINE
23 NEAT
24 FEET
25 FATE

26

F	A	T	H	E	R
A	■	H	■	■	A
R	A	R	E	S	T
M	■	I	■	■	H
E	■	L	■	■	E
R	O	L	L	E	R

27

■	M	■	S	■	T
B	U	T	T	E	R
■	T	■	R	■	A
A	T	T	E	N	D
■	E	■	E	■	E
C	R	A	T	E	R

28 TRUE
29 FLUFF
30 LETTER
31 last
32 sprig
33 gain
34 beaker
35 pains

36	dim	bright
37	mild	harsh
38	wicked	good
39	heat	cool
40	ours	theirs
41	24	48
42	5	11
43	55	22
44	18	7
45	7	2
46	close	quietly
47	mother	supermarket
48	holidays	joined
49	train	stations
50	break	history

51 cupboard
52 goodbye
53 sailor
54 therefore
55 outcast
56 cranial
57 priced
58 carpal
59 agrees
60 trades
61 PUMA
62 FELL
63 CLUE
64 CALM

65 MILE
66 B
67 C
68 WINTER
69 ACEMOPR
70 M
71 KIND
72 SOOT
73 PURE
74 LIFT
75 CORD
76 16
77 19
78 20
79 8
80 7

81	ASLEEP	PLEASE
82	TESTER	STREET
83	SPINAL	PLAINS
84	BITERS	TRIBES
85	CHAPEL	PLEACH

Mixed paper 3

1 stone
2 bumpy
3 barn
4 hand
5 two
6 u
7 q
8 p
9 u
10 t
11 a y i u
12 u o a y
13 a o u i
14 u i a a
15 TEAM
16 BASK
17 CAMP
18 LONG
19 STAR
20 FLOW
21 e
22 p
23 z
24 t
25 g
26 p
27 g
28 l
29 a
30 b

31	eight	equals
32	traffic	forwards
33	killed	chickens
34	rained	muddy
35	haircut	older

36 r 4 c 8
37 b r = 4 c =
38 b 4 r = c 8

39 LAPSE
40 APPLES
41 LM   PQ
42 Yz   Uz
43 IJ   JK
44 ZB   BD
45 CX   GT
46 10   16
47 16   16
48 5   25
49 11   16
50 6   48
51 playground rain wet
52 Yesterday visit hospital
53 types fish sea
54 car car park shops
55 door open inside
56 seem
57 best
58 hall
59 tour
60 very
61 lay   purge
62 quit   every
63 ample   hairs
64 beak   drove
65 water   fiend
66 fraction   part
67 uncle   son
68 March   autumn
69 orange   cereal
70 five   one
71 C
72 E
73 A
74 D
75 B
76 DOTE   DOVE
77 DAMP   DAME
78 ROSY   ROSE
79 LANE   LAND
80 MILE   MALE
81 cereals
82 tools
83 colours
84 computer
85 can

Mixed paper 4

1 bran
2 stained
3 bought
4 hated
5 stand
6 tribe
7 flower
8 dances
9 chives
10 solvent
11 18
12 24
13 23
14 A
15 C
16 ignite, light
17 dwell, live
18 easy, simple
19 lift, elevate
20 under, below
21 strong
22 evil
23 cooled
24 lean
25 sane
26 godfather
27 background
28 into
29 overboard
30 behold
31 FOUR
32 NINE
33 ZERO
34 FIVE
35 F H H G U
36 blew
37 them
38 feel
39 chap
40 this
41 fire
42 ward
43 out
44 gold
45 man
46 BLOW
47 TINT
48 GOLD
49 HOLE
50 HARD
51 brick   glass
52 calm   call
53 four   man
54 road   rails
55 chapter   verse
56 62   102
57 2   15
58 5   7
59 15   8
60 25   17
61 JOKE
62 EARN
63 GRIT
64 HALO
65 KING
66 en
67 er
68 ee
69 st
70 es
71 hot roads melting
72 through quietly hear
73 slipped icy arm
74 track uneven puddles
75 colour red post boxes
76 V J T Q Y
77 N Y Q R Y
78 YEARN
79 APRIL
80 MARCH
81 BOLIVIA
82 BULGARIA
83 BOTSWANA
84

```
B A N T E R
  T   R   E
R O W I N G
  N   L   E
M E R L I N
  S   S   T
```

85

```
P A R A D E
A   E   R
S A L T E D
T   I   D
R A V A G E
Y   E   E
```

Mixed paper 5

1 leave in place
2 watched programme cities
3 shining brightly window
4 book reading exciting
5 shop rotten buy
6 same
7 dry
8 inner
9 low
10 vanish
11 autumn   leaves
12 bonfire   night
13 football   sport
14 pencil   working
15 capital   England
16 4 9 3 5
17 6 1 3 5 4
18 2 1 4 7 5
19 HEDGE
20 CABBAGE
21 n
22 h
23 l
24 d
25 s
26 ROSE
27 SIRE
28 SHIP
29 HEAR
30 THIN
31 ignite
32 dragon
33 drained
34 crusts
35 shelter
36 22
37 A
38 B
39 24
40 D
41 brush   spade
42 see   ear
43 punishment reward
44 pursue   trust
45 paw   talon
46 D
47 G
48 R
49 N
50 H
51 LICE
52 BEAR
53 FULL
54 RAIN
55 RAGE
56 C B P M W
57 NIGHT
58 AWAKE
59 M J F I S
60 Q N T S X
61 finish   start
62 deep   shallow
63 clean   dirty
64 blunt   sharp
65 pull   push
66 fore
67 wire
68 hub
69 suck
70 dare
71 CHIP
72 BRED
73 MEAN   74 HUSH
75 CHAT   76 rear
77 mesh   78 then
79 tone   80 sour
81 A8   B9
82 DJ   PB
83 IR   HT
84 DE   FG
85 YE   AC

Mixed paper 6

1 LEAF
2 WASP
3 DIRT
4 EACH
5 PLEA

Bond Verbal Reasoning Assessment Papers Stretch 10–11+ years

6

D	E	B	A	T	E
O		O		A	
U	N	R	O	L	L
B		R		K	
L	O	O	K	E	D
E		W		D	

7

T	A	L	E	N	T
A		E		I	
V	O	T	I	N	G
E		H		E	
R	E	A	C	T	S
N		L		Y	

8 C
9 P
10 R
11 PX RZ
12 MM NP
13 PP VY
14 ZA YB
15 BQ AW
16 SNOWY
17 H Z U D T
18 ROADS
19 Z E B T P
20 R T R H N
21 4 4
22 1 2
23 12 21
24 11 8
25 11 9
26 V
27 W
28 Y
29 Z
30 W
31 A
32 2
33 D
34 C
35 one
36 pod
37 grave
38 won
39 bake
40 than
41 charm, allure
42 fix, attach
43 insane, senseless
44 move, shift
45 stick, adhere
46 side
47 high
48 man
49 horse
50 slip
51 over
52 pet

53 quick
54 grey
55 ram
56 bacon snipe
57 with chair
58 stale bringing
59 chin bread
60 nigh meant
61 height
62 tall
63 lesser
64 trap
65 pane
66 LAMENT MENTAL
67 REPORT PORTER
68 DRIEST STRIDE
69 LATENT TALENT
70 LEADER DEALER
71 HARD
72 TALE
73 DISH
74 COME
75 DEAD
76 B B U F R
77 STEEP
78 F S Z J M
79 STALL
80 E V Y A X
81 they
82 down 83 reel
84 oral 85 chop

Mixed paper 7

1 stale 2 cat
3 trait 4 to
5 chum 6 way
7 light 8 pine
9 slack 10 wind
11 great 12 green
13 ball

14

T	I	P	T	O	E
	C		O		N
P	I	C	K	L	E
	C		E		R
	L		N		G
F	E	I	S	T	Y

15

P	R	A	Y	E	R
A		O		E	
T		U		A	
S	T	A	T	U	S
L		H		O	
S	E	A	S	O	N

16 HAND
17 HARD
18 DASH
19 SAND

20 S Z T G
21 TALE TALL
22 RIFT RAFT
23 SHOW SLOW
24 SPUR SPUN
25 RAVE HAVE
26 bare, naked
27 climb, ascend
28 steal, rob
29 pig, hog
30 pardon, forgive
31 FF JH
32 ZE BI
33 TB KA
34 ZX XA
35 ZA AZ
36 care
37 for
38 house
39 cart
40 leg
41 E R A H V
42 O N T D T
43 GIRLS
44 VILLA 45 STRAW
46 STORK 47 SWIFT
48 A 49 G
50 N 51 RICK
52 ABLE 53 ICED
54 RAKE 55 EDGE
56 bust 57 also
58 tour 59 them
60 ours 61 support
62 foot 63 times
64 toenail 65 case
66 F 67 L
68 O 69 E
70 O 71 th
72 ex 73 se
74 ea 75 al
76 XW 77 ID
78 EH 79 MN
80 JQ 81 NODE
82 SALE 83 SITE
84 FROG 85 SUCH

Mixed paper 8

1 X Z U D S
2 HOSES
3 BLACK
4 Q J Y F C
5 G M P P E
6 wing
7 black
8 hide
9 bolt
10 key
11 FAME FUME
12 TWIN THIN
13 WASH WISH
14 FACE FADE

15 MOON NOON
16 DE
17 DW
18 DH
19 VB
20 WB
21 R T F D O
22 H T W K V
23 JEANS
24 Q X M S B
25 LARGE
26 ate
27 lime
28 keep
29 slit
30 overt
31 sparkling
32 play
33 uneven 34 bruise
35 cut 36 OMEN
37 WEEP 38 VEST
39 TOMB 40 NAIL
41 TART 42 LASH
43 RIPE 44 AGED
45 HOSE 46 ours
47 land 48 herb
49 rest 50 then
51 XX TT
52 MO LL
53 MP YB
54 TY IJ
55 RB GV
56 chair, sofa
57 purple, violet
58 leopard, lion
59 kind, sort
60 gesture, signal
61 N
62 H
63 T
64 BLACK
65 GREY
66 red
67 green
68 Micah
69 Sarah
70 Sam
71 ar
72 op
73 ch
74 ce
75 un
76 skin
77 apostrophe
78 centimetre
79 bread
80 metal
81 hound
82 show
83 side
84 pay
85 man

Example   mea (<u>t</u>) able   fi (<u>t</u>) ub

21 bit (_) ach   hat (_) very   **24** sea (_) op   mea (_) win

22 fla (_) ony   tra (_) et   **25** dra (_) host   sin (_) et

23 qui (_) ip   buz (_) oo

Which one letter can be added to the front of all of these words to make new words?

Example <u>c</u>are   <u>c</u>at   <u>c</u>rate   <u>c</u>all

26 __art   __each   __arched   __ink

27 __asp   __rate   __lad   __row

28 __and   __ink   __ate   __imp

29 __we   __sleep   __cross   __head

30 __lock   __low   __ear   __army

Rearrange the muddled words in capital letters so that each sentence makes sense.

Example   There are sixty SNODCES <u>seconds</u> in a UTMINE <u>minute</u>.

31 HTEIG _____________ plus seven QLSUEA _____________ fifteen.

32 The green CTRIAFF _____________ light allows cars to move WFRODSAR _____________.

33 Last night, a fox LDELKI _____________ our HCCKNEIS _____________.

34 As it has DRAINE _____________ hard, the park will be very YDUMD _____________.

35 Maisy's new RCHTUIA _____________ makes her look much DLORE _____________.

If the code for STAPLE is c 8 4 b r =, what are the codes for the following words?

36 LAST   _____________   **38** PALEST   _____________

37 PLEASE   _____________

Using the same code, what do the following codes stand for?

39 r 4 b c = _____________   **40** 4 b b r = c _____________

Find the two missing pairs of letters in the following sequences.

A B C D E F G H I J K L M N O P Q R S T U V W X Y Z

Example	CQ	DP	EQ	FP	<u>GQ</u>	<u>HP</u>
41 JK		__	NO	__	RS	TU
42 Zz		__	Xz	Wz	Vz	__
43 GH	HI	__	__		KL	LM
44 __	AC	__		CE	DF	EG
45 __	DW	EV	FU		__	HS

Find the two missing numbers in the following sequences.

Example	2	4	6	8	<u>10</u>	<u>12</u>
46 7		__	13	__	19	22
47 15		__	__	14	17	12
48 __	10	15	20	__	30	
49 1	2	4	7	__	__	
50 3		__	12	24	__	96

Complete the following sentences by selecting the most sensible word from each group of words given in the brackets. Underline the words selected.

Example   The (<u>children</u>, boxes, foxes) carried the (houses, <u>books</u>, steps) home from the (greengrocer, <u>library</u>, factory).

51 We cannot go out into the (playground, classroom, bedroom) as it is pouring with (fire, rain, snow) and we will get very (tired, hot, wet).

52 (Yesterday, Tomorrow, Today) afternoon we went to (annoy, climb, visit) a friend who is sick in (hospital, cinema, fire station).

53 There are many (types, cans, envelopes) of (cows, fish, paper) that live in the (house, sea, jar).

54 Mum parked the (horse, car, train) in the (pond, car park, hedge) next to the (shops, swan, kettle).

55 As the (book, door, mouth) was (wide, open, speaking) she went (inside, outside, over) without knocking.

Find the four-letter word hidden at the end of one word and the beginning of the next word. The order of the letters may not be changed.

Example   We had bat<u>s and</u> balls. <u>sand</u>

56 Please empty your rubbish bin over here. _______________

57 The cat is asleep and doesn't want to be stroked. _______________

58 At break time we played with all the little children. _______________

59 We met our new next door neighbours at the party. _______________

60 I could see your swing over your garden fence. _______________   ◯ 5

Move one letter from the first word and add it to the second word to make two new words.

Example   hunt   sip   <u>hut</u>   <u>snip</u>

61 play   urge   _______________   _______________

62 quite   very   _______________   _______________

63 sample   hair   _______________   _______________

64 break   dove   _______________   _______________

65 waiter   fend   _______________   _______________   ◯ 5

Underline the two words which are the odd ones out in the following groups of words.

Example   black   <u>king</u>   purple   green   <u>house</u>

66 whole	fraction	entire	complete	part
67 uncle	wife	daughter	grandmother	son
68 Monday	March	Saturday	autumn	Friday
69 orange	cauliflower	carrot	cereal	courgette
70 sixteen	five	one	eight	four

◯ 5

On a garden rockery, there were seven stones. Under each stone lived a different type of small animal. From the clues and the diagram, work out where each type of animal lived.

LEFT				RIGHT	
A				SNAILS	TOP
	B		C		
CENTIPEDES		D		E	BOTTOM

The snails were not directly above the woodlice.

The beetles were on a row somewhere above the woodlice.

The centipedes were on the same row as the worms.

The earwigs were on the same row as the slugs, which are closer to the centipedes than the earwigs.

71 earwigs	______________	**74** woodlice	______________
72 worms	______________	**75** slugs	______________
73 beetles	______________		

Change the first word into the last word, by changing one letter at a time and making two new, different words in the middle.

Example CASE   <u>CASH</u>   <u>WASH</u>   WISH

76 VOTE	______________	______________	DIVE
77 RAMP	______________	______________	DIME
78 COSY	______________	______________	ROVE
79 LATE	______________	______________	LEND
80 MILK	______________	______________	KALE

Underline the one word in the brackets which will go equally well with each of the words outside the brackets.

Example   word, paragraph, sentence   (pen, cap, <u>letter</u>, top, stop)

81 wheat, oats, bran   (breakfast, cereals, grass, bread, milk)

82 spanner, hammer, saw   (tools, nail, screw, wood, mend)

83 indigo, brown, red   (paint, rainbow, sky, lights, colours)

84 keys, mouse, screen   (lock, trap, wide, computer, mobile)

85 mug, waste paper basket, barrel   (roll, tea, watering can, ball, cannot)

Now go to the Progress Chart to record your score!   Total   85

Mixed paper 4

Remove one letter from the word in capital letters to leave a new word. The meaning of the new word is given in the clue.

Example AUNT an insect <u>ant</u>

1 BRAND fibre ______________

2 STRAINED marked ______________

3 BROUGHT purchased ______________

4 HEATED loathed ______________

5 STRAND upright ______________   5

Underline the one word in each group which **can be made** from the letters of the word in capital letters.

Example CHAMPION camping notch peach cramp <u>chimp</u>

6 BRIGHTEN gender rights tribe better nightie

7 POWERFUL flower proof parole leper prefer

8 DISTANCE canter stains dances stands insist

9 VEHICLES sieves sleek leaves wheels chives

10 TELEVISION notelet hotels notice solvent noises   5

If t = 4, c = 7, r = 3, a = 1, l = 5, e = 6 and w = 2, find the sum of these words when the letters are added together.

11 crawl ______________   13 wallet ______________

12 crater ______________   3

Read the first two statements and then underline one of the four options below that must be true.

14 'Madrid is the capital of Spain. Spain is in Europe.'

   A Madrid is a European city.

   B England is in Europe.

   C The euro is the currency for much of Europe.

   D People from Spain speak Spanish.

15 'A robin is a type of bird. Birds have feathers.'

   A Robins are good at flying.   **C** Robins have feathers.

   B Robins have red breasts.   **D** All birds are robins.

Underline the pair of words which are the most similar in meaning.

Example come, go   <u>roams, wanders</u>   fear, fare

16 ignite, light   pale, dark   night, day

17 life, death   dwell, live   fetch, carry

18 true, false   easy, simple   tough, clear

19 lift, elevate   drop, leave   come, go

20 up, down   over, through   under, below

Find the word that is opposite in meaning to the word in capital letters and that rhymes with the second word.

Example SHARP   front   <u>blunt</u>

21 FRAIL   long   __________

22 GOOD   weevil   __________

23 HEATED   ruled   __________

24 PLUMP   seen   __________

25 CRAZY   drain   __________

Underline two words, one from each group, that go together to form a new word. The word in the first group always comes first.

Example (hand, <u>green</u>, for)   (light, <u>house</u>, sure)

26 (good, god, grade)   (further, father, future)

27 (back, four, head)   (plain, ground, grass)

28 (in, and, who)   (to, be, how)

29 (over, oven, order)   (line, law, board)

30 (in, out, be)   (hold, hive, port)

If the code for STORM is T S P Q N, match the right code to each word given below.

ZERO   FOUR   FIVE   NINE

31 G N V Q   _______________

32 O H O D   _______________

33 A D S N   _______________

34 G H W D   _______________

35 What would EIGHT be, using the same code? _______________

Find the four-letter word hidden at the end of one word and the beginning of the next word. The order of the letters may not be changed.

Example We had bat<u>s and</u> balls. <u>sand</u>

36 Calm down and try explaining in a quiet and sensible way.

____

37 As the weather worsened, the mountains disappeared from view.

____

38 Tea and coffee leave me feeling thirsty. _______________

39 We looked carefully for blemishes on each apple. _______________

40 Conrad left his jacket on the floor of the gym. _______________

Find a word that can be put either in front or at the end of each of the following words to make new, compound words.

Example cast   fall   ward   pour   <u>down</u>

41 cracker   ball   fighter   side   _______________

42 for   back   in   up   _______________

43 doors   back   look   grow   _______________

44 finch   fish   smith   field   _______________

45 age   kind   hood   or   _______________

Change the first word into the last word, by changing one letter at a time and making a new, different word in the middle.

Example CASE   <u>CASH</u>   LASH

46 BROW   _______________   SLOW

47 TINY   _______________   TILT

48 GOOD   _______________   BOLD

49 HOME   _______________   HOLT

50 YARD   _______________   HARK

Complete the following sentences in the best way by choosing one word from each set of brackets.

Example Tall is to (tree, <u>short</u>, colour) as narrow is to (thin, white, <u>wide</u>).

51 House is to (roof, door, brick) as greenhouse is to (glass, small, plants).

52 Belt is to bell as (calm, ramp, find) is to (damp, call, farm).

53 Cat is to (fur, four, mouse) as (man, hat, number) is to two.

54 Lorry is to (big, car, road) as train is to (rails, passenger, ticket).

55 Book is to (chapter, novel, title) as poem is to (verse, word, rhyme).

Find the two missing numbers in the following sequences.

Example 2 4 6 8 <u>10</u> <u>12</u>

56 2 22 42 __ 82 __

57 __ __ 6 13 10 11

58 __ 3 4 5 3 __

59 26 20 __ 11 __ 6

60 29 __ 21 __ 13 9

Look at the first group of three words. The word in the middle has been made from the two other words. Complete the second group of three words in the same way, making a new word in the middle.

Example PAIN IN<u>TO</u> TOOK ALSO <u>SOON</u> ONLY

61 JERK PORK PONY MAKE _____________ JOIN

62 CLAW LAWN NOTE WEAR _____________ NAIL

63 HOOF FISH SIFT TANG _____________ IRON

64 CALL ALSO SOLD WHAT _____________ LOOK

65 LIMB BONE ZONE HUSK _____________ WING

Find the two letters that will end the first word and start the second word.

Example pas (<u>ta</u>) ste

66 brok (__ __) joy

67 tend (__ __) ect

68 agr (__ __) rie

69 fir (__ __) amp

70 bus (__ __) say

Complete the following sentences by selecting the most sensible word from each group of words given in the brackets. Underline the words selected.

Example The (<u>children</u>, boxes, foxes) carried the (houses, <u>books</u>, steps) home from the (greengrocer, <u>library</u>, factory).

71 It is so (hot, cold, rainy) today that the tarmac on the (roads, bikes, deer) is (swimming, crying, melting).

72 The lioness crept (up, with, through) the long grass so (quietly, loudly, kindly) the deer did not see or (touch, hear, laugh) her coming.

73 Poor Alvina (slipped, laughed, sang) on the (icy, green, pretty) step and fell and broke her (father, water, arm).

74 The (track, elevator, ladder) to the farm was rough and (level, uneven, easy) with large, muddy (puddles, spiders, boots).

75 My favourite (bed, colour, cat) is (high, spotty, red) like the colour of (post boxes, caravans, pillows).

5

76 If the code for CATCH is E C V E J, what is the code for THROW?

____

77 If the code for LUNCH is J S L A F, what is the code for PASTA?

____

78 If the code for WANTS is Z D Q W V, what does B H D U Q stand for?

____

3

If the code for AUGUST is Z V F V R U, what do the following codes stand for?

79 Z Q Q J K _______________   **80** L B Q D G _______________

2

BULGARIA   BELGIUM   BOTSWANA   BOLIVIA   BURUNDI

If these countries are put in alphabetical order, which comes:

81 second? _________ **82** fourth? _________ **83** after Bolivia? _________

3

Fill in the crosswords so that all the given words are included. You have been given one letter as a clue in each crossword.

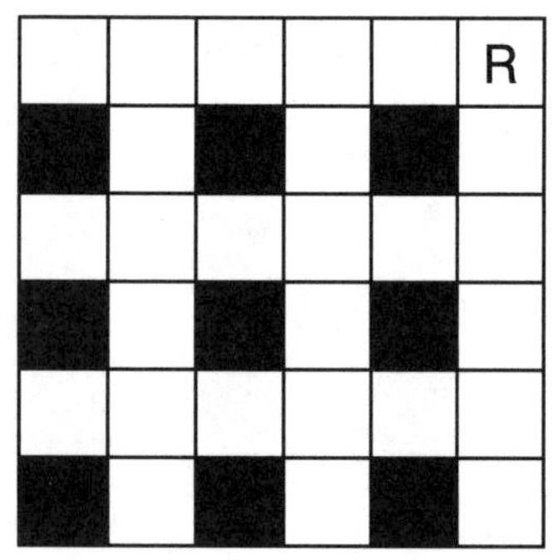

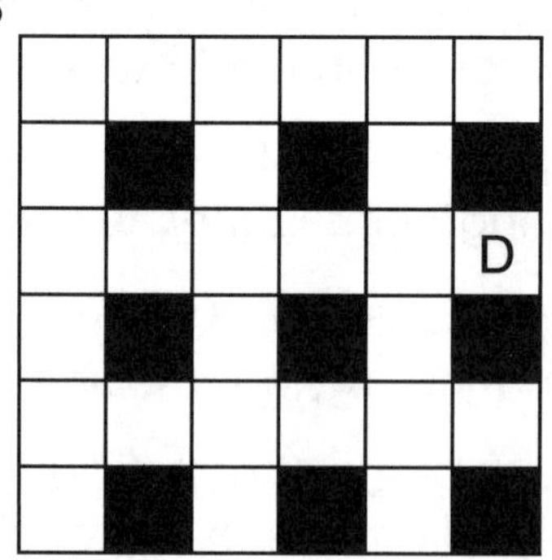

REGENT   BANTER   TRILLS
ROWING   MERLIN   ATONES

PASTRY   PARADE   DREDGE
RAVAGE   SALTED   RELIVE

2

Now go to the Progress Chart to record your score!   Total **85**

Mixed paper 5

Complete the following sentences by selecting the most sensible word from each group of words given in the brackets. Underline the words selected.

Example   The (<u>children</u>, boxes, foxes) carried the (houses, <u>books</u>, steps) home from the (greengrocer, <u>library</u>, factory).

1 Please don't (leave, find, jump) me alone (in, through, over) this strange (place, colour, wolf).

2 Yesterday we (ate, watched, threw) an interesting (pizza, programme, spear) on animals living in our (cities, buckets, socks).

3 The moon is (shining, calling, falling) really (suddenly, brightly, quickly) through my bedroom (wall, road, window).

4 The (book, garage, bird) I am (reading, flying, mending) at the moment is very (exciting, swimming, driving).

5 The fruit in the (shop, bridge, cage) was either unripe or (rotten, unkind, pink) so my mother did not (eat, buy, wish) it.

5

Find the word that is opposite in meaning to the word in capital letters and that rhymes with the second word.

Example   SHARP   front   <u>blunt</u>

6 DIFFERENT   blame   __________

7 WET   fly   __________

| 8 OUTER | dinner | _____________ |
| 9 HIGH | sew | _____________ |
| 10 APPEAR | banish | _____________ | 5

Rearrange the muddled words in capital letters so that each sentence makes sense.

Example There are sixty SNODCES <u>seconds</u> in a UTMINE <u>minute</u>.

11 In AUUMNT _______________ many trees lose their VSELAE

_______________.

12 The BFRENIO _______________ burned brightly against the INHGT

_______________ sky.

13 BFLTOALO _______________ is my favourite PTORS _______________ at
our school.

14 Her CLIPNE _______________ kept breaking as she was GNIWRKO

_______________.

15 London is the PTLACAI _______________ city of GLAENDN

_______________. 5

If the code for BEAD is 2 5 1 4, what are the codes for the following words?

16 DICE   _______________   18 BADGE   _______________

17 FACED   _______________

Using the same code, what do the following codes stand for?

19 8 5 4 7 5 _______________   20 3 1 2 2 1 7 5 _______________ 5

Find the letter that will end the first word and start the second word.

Example   drow (<u>n</u>) ought

21 year (___) or   24 hee (___) oor

22 bus (___) orror   25 wa (___) wan

23 vea (___) ove 5

Change the first word into the last word, by changing one letter at a time and
making a new, different word in the middle.

Example CASE   <u>CASH</u>   LASH

26	HOSE	__________	ROBE
27	SURE	__________	FIRE
28	WHIP	__________	SLIP
29	GEAR	__________	HEAP
30	CHIN	__________	THAN

5

Underline the one word in each group which **cannot be made** from the letters of the word in capital letters.

Example STATIONERY stone tyres ration <u>nation</u> noisy

31	LIGHTNING	glint	night	ignite	thing	tiling
32	GRANDEUR	danger	gander	ranger	dragon	grader
33	SPRAINED	drapes	rinsed	rained	drained	spared
34	CREATURES	steer	crusts	curate	traces	secret
35	BATTLESHIP	spittle	thistle	shape	tables	shelter

5

In a test at school out of 35, pupil A got 24 right while pupil B got 17 wrong. C got 10 less than D who got 4 more than B. E got half of A's score.

36 How many did D get right? __________

37 Who did the best? __________

38 Who got 6 more marks than C? __________

39 How many marks did C and E score when their totals are added together? __________

40 Who did better than B but not as well as A? __________

5

Complete the following sentences in the best way by choosing one word from each set of brackets.

Example Tall is to (tree, <u>short</u>, colour) as narrow is to (thin, white, <u>wide</u>).

41 Broom is to (brush, mop, hammer) as shovel is to (nail, fork, spade).

42 Eye is to (lash, see, face) as (ear, hair, foot) is to hear.

43 Crime is to (criminal, punishment, robber) as a good deed is to (reward, thief, problem).

44 Chase is to (pursue, catch, keep) as believe in is to (lie, trust, pray).

45 Wolf is to (howl, paw, hunt) as eagle is to (soar, talon, beak).

5

42

If the letters of the word TREADING are put into alphabetical order, which comes:

46 second? _____ **48** seventh? _____

47 fourth? _____

If the letters of the word CHAMPION are put into alphabetical order, which comes:

49 sixth? _____ **50** third? _____

Find the four-letter word which can be added to the letters in capitals to make a new word. The new word will complete the sentence sensibly.

Example They enjoyed the BCAST. <u>ROAD</u>

51 Please may I have another S of cake? _____

52 Father Christmas is pictured with a bushy white D. _____

53 HOPEY it will stop raining soon. _____

54 Deserts are dry, arid places with little FALL. _____

55 My father has a workshop in the GA. _____

56 If the code for SLEEP is Q M C F N, what is the code for EARLY?

_____

57 Using the same code, what does L J E I R stand for? _____

58 If the code for DREAM is C S D B L, what does Z X Z L D stand for?

_____

59 Using the same code, what is the code for NIGHT? _____

60 If the code for TIGER is Y N L J W, what is the code for LIONS?

_____

Underline the two words, one from each group, which are the most opposite in meaning.

Example (dawn, <u>early</u>, wake) (<u>late</u>, stop, sunrise)

61 (surprise, finish, book) (end, start, paper)

62 (deep, broad, high) (steep, shallow, wide)

63 (grubby, clean, messy) (dirty, chaos, dump)

64 (pencil, chalk, blunt) (pen, sharp, feeble)

65 (pull, heave, choose) (press, push, select)

Change the first word of the third pair in the same way as the other pairs to give a new word.

Example   bind, hind   bare, hare   but, <u>hut</u>

66 comb, come   wand, wane   form, ________________

67 type, tyre   pant, part   wine, ________________

68 come, hum   with, hut   jibe, ________________

69 lack, luck   tack, tuck   sack, ________________

70 leap, pale   deaf, fade   read, ________________   5

Look at the first group of three words. The word in the middle has been made from the two other words. Complete the second group of three words in the same way, making a new word in the middle.

Example   PA<u>IN</u>   INTO   <u>TO</u>OK   ALSO   <u>SOON</u>   ONLY

71 BATH   THIN   WIND   RICH   ______________ WIPE

72 FORT   TRIM   SLIM   KERB   ______________ SPED

73 PEAR   READ   DAMP   GERM   ______________ NAVY

74 ENDS   SHOE   HOME   HIGH   ______________ USED

75 KITE   TERM   MORE   MUCH   ______________ TRAP   5

Find the four-letter word hidden at the end of one word and the beginning of the next word. The order of the letters may not be changed.

Example   We had bat<u>s and</u> balls. <u>sand</u>

76 Where are your clean clothes, Javin? ______________

77 Tania will not be allowed to come shopping with you on Friday.

____

78 A train clattered by noisily through the new level crossing.

____

79 Paul put one of his paintings in an art exhibition. ______________

80 A squirrel visits our bird table to gobble all the bird food. ______________   5

Find the two missing pairs of letters in the following sequences.

A B C D E F G H I J K L M N O P Q R S T U V W X Y Z

Example   CQ   DP   EQ   FP   <u>GQ</u>   <u>HP</u>

81	Y6	Z7	__	__	C10	D11
82	__	GH	JF	MD	__	SZ
83	HP	__	__	IV	HX	IZ
84	AB	BC	CD	__	EF	__
85	__	__	CA	EY	GW	IU

Mixed paper 6

Look at the first group of three words. The word in the middle has been made from the two other words. Complete the second group of three words in the same way, making a new word in the middle.

Example   PA<u>IN</u>   INTO   <u>TO</u>OK   ALSO   <u>SOON</u>   ONLY

1 POSH   HOOP   SORT   FAIL   ______________   FERN

2 BUSY   MUST   MINT   GASH   ______________   WEEP

3 LOOK   KEEP   PEEK   LOAD   ______________   TRIP

4 REEL   FEAR   LOAF   HOAX   ______________   NICE

5 SNAP   DRIP   BIRD   PUMA   ______________   HELP

Fill in the crosswords so that all the given words are included. You have been given one letter as a clue in each crossword.

6

BORROW   LOOKED   UNROLL

TALKED   DOUBLE   DEBATE

7

REACTS   TAVERN   TALENT

VOTING   NINETY   LETHAL

If the letters of the word PICTURES are put into alphabetical order, which comes:

8 first? _____   **9** fourth? _____   **10** fifth? _____

Find the two missing pairs of letters in the following sequences.

A B C D E F G H I J K L M N O P Q R S T U V W X Y Z

Example CQ   DP   EQ   FP   <u>GQ</u>   <u>HP</u>

11 __   __   TB   VD   XF   ZH

12 MK   NL   __   NN   MO   __

13 NM   __   RS   TV   __   XB

14 CX   BY   AZ   __   __   XC

15 __   GM   LI   QE   VA   __

16 If the code for IGLOO is K F N N Q, what does U M Q V A stand for?

____

17 If the code for FENCE is G D O B F, what is the code for GATES?

____

18 If the code for CROSS is D S P T T, what does S P B E T stand for?

____

19 If the code for BITES is Y F Q B P, what is the code for CHEWS?

____

20 If the code for TEACH is V D C B J, what is the code for PUPIL?

____

Find the two missing numbers in the following sequences.

Example 2 4 6 8 <u>10</u> <u>12</u>

21 8 2 6 3 __ __ 2 5   **24** 2 __ 4 8 6 5 __ 2

22 __ __ 4 7 11 16 22 29   **25** 10 13 __ 11 12 __ 13 7

23 3 6 9 __ 15 18 __ 24

If Z = 3, Y = 5, W = 10, V = 2 and U = 4, what are the values of these calculations? Write each answer as a letter.

26 $(Z + Y) - (W - U) =$ _____   **28** $\dfrac{(Y + Z + W + V)}{U} =$ _____

27 $(U^2 - Z^2) + Z \quad =$ _____

29 $(VYZ) \div W =$ _____   **30** $ZW - YU =$ _____

At a football match, six friends all wore their red supporters' shirts. A and B wore hats but no scarves. C, F and E wore hats and scarves. B and D and E had flags and hats. A and C carried whistles.

31 Who had a whistle but no scarf? ________________

32 How many friends wore hats and scarves but no whistles?

____

33 Who, besides A and B, did not have a scarf? ________________

34 Who had a hat, scarf and whistle? ________________

35 How many wore scarves and carried flags? ________________

Change the first word of the third pair in the same way as the other pairs to give a new word.

Example   bind, hind   bare, hare   but, <u>hut</u>

36 gasp, gap   camp, cap   pond, _____________

37 knit, knave   slow, slave   gruel, _____________

38 pot, top   nit, tin   now, _____________

39 food, fade   moon, mane   book, _____________

40 crime, mean   stale, lean   broth, _____________

Underline the pair of words which are the most similar in meaning.

Example   come, go   <u>roams, wanders</u>   fear, fare

41 charm, allure   repel, avoid   dazzle, subdue

42 fix, attach   sew, needle   stitch, tapestry

43 mad, sane   insane, senseless   common, sense

44 remain, go   below, behind   move, shift

45 glue, tape   stick, adhere   paste, solid

Find a word that can be put either in front or at the end of each of the following words to make new, compound words.

Example   cast   fall   ward   pour   <u>down</u>

46	out	in	be	a	_______________
47	lighter	land	ball	way	_______________
48	hole	age	servant	trap	_______________
49	play	fly	power	back	_______________
50	stream	per	ping	way	_______________

Underline the one word in the brackets which will go equally well with both sets of words outside the brackets.

Example rush, attack   cost, fee   (price, hasten, strike, <u>charge</u>, money)

51 done, finished   cricketing term   (over, complete, wicket, century, ball)

52 domestic animal   stroke, pat   (cat, rabbit, fondle, pet, dog)

53 fast, swift   intelligent, sharp   (quick, rapid, clever, bright, cool)

54 a colour   dull, nondescript   (blue, yellow, black, grey, brown)

55 male sheep   pack, stuff   (ram, ewe, thrust, crash, strike)

Move one letter from the first word and add it to the second word to make two new words.

Example hunt   sip   <u>hut</u>   <u>snip</u>

56	beacon	snip	_____________	_____________
57	witch	hair	_____________	_____________
58	stable	ringing	_____________	_____________
59	chain	bred	_____________	_____________
60	night	mean	_____________	_____________

Underline the one word in the brackets which will go with the word outside the brackets in the same way as the first two words go together.

Example good, better   bad, (naughty, worst, <u>worse</u>, nasty)

61 wide, width   high, (height, higher, highest, low)

62 tight, loose	short, (small, shrunk, tall, even)
63 hottest, hotter	least, (less, hot, lesser, lesson)
64 tops, spot	part, (past, trap, rapt, step)
65 calm, palm	cane, (pare, pane, care, cape)

Underline the two words in each line which are made from the same letters.

Example TAP   PET   <u>TEA</u>   POT   <u>EAT</u>

66 PARADE	DEARER	LAMENT	MENTAL	PARENT
67 REPORT	PORTER	TREATS	STREET	STRIPE
68 UGLIER	GRUELS	DRIEST	STRIDE	GUESTS
69 LATENT	TALENT	STALER	RESTED	TRUEST
70 LEADER	DREAMS	SMEARED	INDEED	DEALER

Change the first word into the last word, by changing one letter at a time and making a new, different word in the middle.

Example CASE   <u>CASH</u>   LASH

71 YARD	_____________	HAND
72 TAPE	_____________	TALK
73 FISH	_____________	DASH
74 COMB	_____________	CORE
75 DEAF	_____________	READ

The code for BREAK is A S D B J. Use this code to answer the following questions.

76 Which of these codes is the right one for CAVES: B B U F R or B B W D T? _____________

77 Which of these words is the right one for R U D F O: STEEP or STEER? _____________

78 Which of these codes is the right one for GRAIN: F S Z J M or F S Z J O? _____________

79 Which of these words is the right one for R U Z M K: STALK or STALL? _____________

80 Which of these codes is the right one for FUZZY: E V Y Y X or
E V Y A X? _______________

Find the four-letter word hidden in each sentence. Each begins at the end
of one word and the beginning of another word, and can cover two or three
words. The order of the letters may not be changed.

Example We had ba<u>ts and</u> balls. <u>sand</u>

81 To tremendous applause, the young players ran onto the pitch.
____

82 We apologised when we broke the glass in the classroom window next
to the playground. _______________

83 I counted three large fish swimming slowly round the pond.
____

84 After working for a long time in the baking sun, we had a break.
____

85 Please leave the door to the church open, when you leave.
____

Now go to the Progress Chart to record your score!   Total   85

Mixed paper 7

Change the first word of the third pair in the same way as the other pairs to
give a new word.

Example bind, hind   bare, hare   but, <u>hut</u>

1 great, grate   fear, fare   steal, _______________

2 drum, dam   begin, ban   closet, _______________

3 bend, bent   form, fort   trail, _______________

4 beam, me   mesh, he   cost, _______________

5 dust, stud   dame, mead   much, _______________

Underline the one word in the brackets which will go equally well with both
sets of words outside the brackets.

Example rush, attack   cost, fee   (price, hasten, strike,
<u>charge</u>, money)

6 road, path   method, style   (track, way, route, distance, manner)

7 pale, faint   lamp, lantern   (torch, soft, gentle, light, candle)

8 long for, miss   evergreen tree   (fir, yew, pine, yearn, ache)

9 slapdash, lax   limp, loose   (sagging, slack, slow, negligent, careless)

10 air movement   twist, turn   (current, air, wind, loop, snake)

11 excellent, very good   enormous, vast   (large, huge, great, wonderful, fat)

12 unripe, grassy   a colour   (green, blue, yellow, apple, white)

13 sphere, game component   dance, smart party   (cone, rule, ball, disco, game)

Fill in the crosswords so that all the given words are included. You have been given one letter as a clue in each crossword.

14

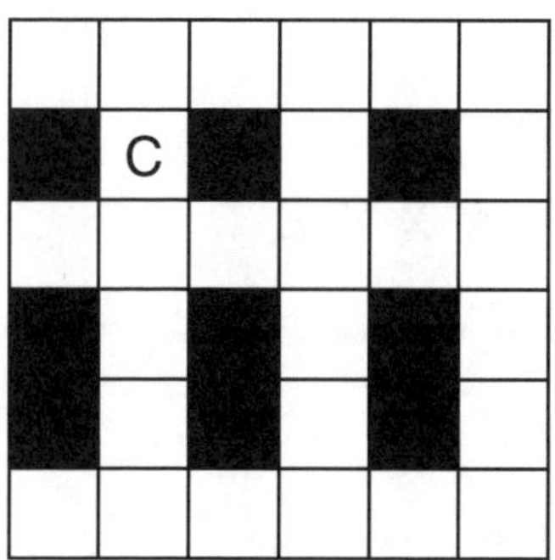

PICKLE TOKENS TIPTOE

FEISTY ENERGY ICICLE

15

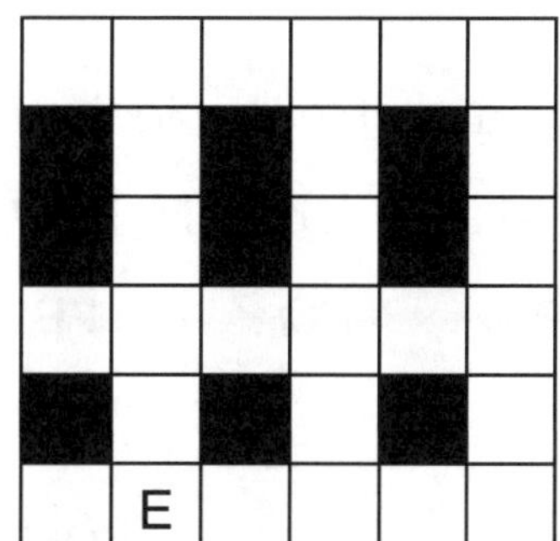

PRAYER RATTLE SEASON

REASON YOUTHS STATUS

If the code for GARAGE is H Z S Z H D, match the right word to each code given below.

     SAND   HAND   HARD   DASH

16 I Z O C   ________________   **18** E Z T G   ________________

17 I Z S C   ________________   **19** T Z O C   ________________

20 Using the same code, what is the code for RASH? ________________

Change the first word into the last word, by changing one letter at a time and making two new, different words in the middle.

Example CASE   <u>CASH</u>   <u>WASH</u>   WISH

21 TAPE   ____________   ____________   TOLL

22 GIFT   ____________   ____________   RAPT

23 SHOD   ____________   ____________   FLOW

24 SLUR   ____________   ____________   SPIN

25 RAGE   ____________   ____________   HIVE

Underline the pair of words which are the most similar in meaning.

Example come, go   <u>roams, wanders</u>   fear, fare

26 bare, naked   clip, short   hold, touch

27 encourage, debate   climb, ascend   high, low

28 time, minute   clock, speed   steal, rob

29 halo, angel   pig, hog   yellow, white

30 pardon, forgive   carry, drop   above, below

Find the two missing pairs of letters in the following sequences.

A B C D E F G H I J K L M N O P Q R S T U V W X Y Z

Example CQ   DP   EQ   FP   <u>GQ</u>   <u>HP</u>

31 __   HG   __   LI   NJ   PK

32 XA   YC   __   AG   __   CK

33 __   __   TZ   KY   TX   KW

34 DR   BU   __   __   VD   TG

35 VE   WD   XC   YB   __   __

Find a word that can be put either in front or at the end of each of the following words to make new, compound words.

Example cast   fall   ward   pour   <u>down</u>

36 free	less	taker	worn	___________
37 bid	give	got	mat	___________
38 hold	break	wife	keeper	___________
39 ridge	wheel	on	horse	___________
40 end	room	work	ally	___________

41 If the code for CRATE is F U D W H, what is the code for BOXES?

____

42 If the code for MOUTH is N N V S I, what is the code for NOSES?

____

43 If the code for CHILD is E G K K F, what does I H T K U stand for?

____

44 If the code for HOUSE is E L R P B, what does S F I I X stand for?

____

45 If the code for BERRY is F I V V C, what does W X V E A stand for?

____

STORK   SWALLOW   SWIFT   SPARROW   STARLING

If these birds are put into alphabetical order, which comes:

46 third? ___________   **47** fifth? ___________

If the letters of the word BREAKING are put into alphabetical order, which comes:

48 first? _____   **50** fourth? _____   **49** seventh? _____

Find the four-letter word which can be added to the letters in capitals to make a new word. The new word will complete the sentence sensibly.

Example They enjoyed the BCAST. <u>ROAD</u>

51 Matt scored fifty runs in the CET match at school. ___________

52 Supper's ready; so please lay the T! ___________

53 Mary SL her birthday cake into twelve pieces with a sharp knife.

____

54 Although he slammed on the BS, Aidan's bike crashed into the wall.

____

55 Our garden H badly needs clipping. ___________

Find the four-letter word hidden at the end of one word and the beginning of the next word. The order of the letters may not be changed.

Example We had bat**s and** balls. <u>sand</u>

56 We went by bus to the Houses of Parliament. ________________

57 Sixty six divided by sixty six equals one. ________________

58 We need to collect our tickets from the bus station. ________________

59 The trees by the lake dropped their leaves into the murky water.

____

60 Our school dinner lady is friendly and helpful. ________________

Underline the one word in the brackets which will go with the word outside the brackets in the same way as the first two words go together.

Example good, better   bad, (naughty, worst, <u>worse</u>, nasty)

61 lift, raise   sustain, (support, carry, elevate, meet)

62 finger, toe   hand, (nail, digit, arm, foot)

63 melon, lemon   mites, (mates, stamp, times, smite)

64 cat, claw   person, (foot, toenail, heel, toe)

65 gnome, game   chose, (case, hose, cosy, chase)

If the letters of the word FLAMINGO are put into alphabetical order, which comes:

66 second? _____   **67** fifth? _____   **68** eighth? _____

If the letters of the word SECONDLY are put into alphabetical order, which comes:

69 third? _____   **70** sixth? _____

Find the two letters that will end the first word and start the second word.

Example pas (<u>ta</u>) ste

71 you (__ __) an   **74** ar (__ __) rth

72 fl (__ __) it   **75** op (__ __) low

73 brui (__ __) al

Find the missing letters. The alphabet has been written out to help you.

A B C D E F G H I J K L M N O P Q R S T U V W X Y Z

Example   AB is to CD as PQ is to <u>RS</u>.

76 UT is to SR as ZY is to __.

77 FA is to GB as HC is to __.

78 MN is to LO as FG is to __.

79 BB to EF as JJ is to __.

80 GT is to HS as IR is to __.

Look at the first group of three words. The word in the middle has been made from the two other words. Complete the second group of three words in the same way, making a new word in the middle.

Example   PA<u>IN</u>   INTO   <u>T</u>OOK   ALSO   <u>SOON</u>   ONLY

81 HARE	LAKE	LOOK	BONE	_____________	NEED
82 VASE	VAST	VENT	SALT	_____________	FAZE
83 QUIZ	PILE	PLEA	THIN	_____________	STEW
84 CORN	CORE	CASE	FROM	_____________	WING
85 TIME	MATE	CALM	CASH	_____________	BUSH

Now go to the Progress Chart to record your score!   Total   85

Mixed paper 8

1 If the code for GLASS is H K B R T, what is the code for WATER?

____

2 If the code for SPRAY is Q N P Y W, what does F M Q C Q stand for?

____

3 If the code for GREEN is I T G G P, what does D N C E M stand for?

____

4 If the code for LAMPS is J C K R Q, what is the code for SHADE?

____

5 If the code for RIVER is S J W F S, what is the code for FLOOD?

____

Underline the one word in the brackets which will go equally well with both sets of words outside the brackets.

Example   rush, attack   cost, fee   (price, hasten, strike, <u>charge</u>, money)

6 bird limb   sport position   (leg, centre, half, wing, forearm)

7 terrible, tragic   a colour   (blue, grim, fateful, black, indigo)

8 animal skin   conceal, shroud   (leather, hide, camouflage, fur, cloak)

9 fastener, bar   run away or eat quickly (gobble, escape, bolt, flee, gorge)

10 vital, critical   lock opener   (crucial, decisive, key, jemmy, bar)

5

Change the first word into the last word, by changing one letter at a time and making two new, different words in the middle.

Example   CASE   <u>CASH</u>   <u>WASH</u>   WISH

11 SAME   ____________   ____________   FUSE

12 TWIG   ____________   ____________   CHIN

13 BASH   ____________   ____________   WITH

14 FACT   ____________   ____________   WADE

15 MOOD   ____________   ____________   NOUN

5

Find the missing letters. The alphabet has been written out to help you.

A B C D E F G H I J K L M N O P Q R S T U V W X Y Z

Example   AB is to CD as PQ is to <u>RS</u>.

16 KL is to IJ as FG is to __.   19 SU is to QW as XZ is to __.

17 AZ is to BY as CX is to __.   20 TY is to UZ as VA is to __.

18 AF is to CG as BG is to __.

5

21 If the code for CROWN is D Q P V O, what is the code for QUEEN?

____

22 If the code for GRAPE is I T C R G, what is the code for FRUIT?

____

23 If the code for SHIRT is O D E N P, what does F A W J O stand for?

____

24 If the code for ARROW is Y S P P U, what is the code for SWORD?

____

25 If the code for SMALL is U L C K N, what does N Z T F G stand for?

____

Change the first word of the third pair in the same way as the other pairs to give a new word.

Example bind, hind   bare, hare   but, <u>hut</u>

26 scrape, cap   cheats, hat   barter, ___________

27 calm, lame   port, rote   film, ___________

28 best, bees   felt, feel   kept, ___________

29 swan, sawn   blot, bolt   silt, ___________

30 churches, chest   larkspur, spurt   undercover, ___________

Underline the one word in the brackets which will go with the word outside the brackets in the same way as the first two words go together.

Example good, better   bad, (naughty, worst, <u>worse</u>, nasty)

31 clear, cloudy   still, (almost, sparkling, gloomy, motionless)

32 battle, fight   game, (football, play, run, think, avoid)

33 plain, patterned   flat, (house, striped, brick, uneven)

34 cut, bleed   bump, (bruise, ramp, water, leg)

35 plump, pup   crust, (rust, rut, cut, cur)

Look at the first group of three words. The word in the middle has been made from the two other words. Complete the second group of three words in the same way, making a new word in the middle.

Example PAIN   INTO   T<u>OO</u>K   ALSO   <u>SOON</u>   ONLY

36 CAME   MEAT   BATH   BOOM   ___________   BENT

37 BACK   JACK   JURY   DEEP   ___________   WING

38 BENT   DENT   DIRT   BEST   ___________   VAIN

| **39** HARM | MARK | KERB | BOAT | _______________ | BOMB |
| **40** KISS | SHIP | HOPE | PINK | _______________ | AXLE |

Find the four-letter word which can be added to the letters in capitals to make a new word. The new word will complete the sentence sensibly.

Example They enjoyed the BCAST. <u>ROAD</u>

41 The racehorses grouped together impatiently, ready to S the race. _______________

42 The blue FING light of the ambulance showed up clearly. _______________

43 The rugby player wore a red and white STD shirt. _______________

44 A tree fell on our house and DAM the roof. _______________

45 T pencils you lent me were all blunt! _______________

Find the four-letter word hidden at the end of one word and the beginning of the next word. The order of the letters may not be changed.

Example We had ba<u>ts and</u> balls. <u>sand</u>

46 Your skull protects your brain from harm. _______________

47 I think those exhibition pictures are colourful and attractive. _______________

48 A fox chased a baby rabbit and scared her badly. _______________

49 Why are stamps so expensive now? _______________

50 The nurse put a plaster cast on his broken arm. _______________

Find the two missing pairs of letters in the following sequences.

A B C D E F G H I J K L M N O P Q R S T U V W X Y Z

Example	CQ	DP	EQ	FP	<u>GQ</u>	<u>HP</u>
51	ZZ	__	VV	__	RR	PP
52	__	LN	MM	__	MK	LJ
53	AD	GJ	__	SV	__	EH
54	__	WV	ZS	CP	FM	__
55	MD	__	WZ	BX	__	LT

Underline the pair of words which are the most similar in meaning.

Example come, go   <u>roams, wanders</u>   fear, fare

56 bed, window   chair, sofa   table, cupboard

57 red, green   blue, orange   purple, violet

58 leopard, lion   monkey, bear   fish, bird

59 kind, sort   hold, drop   behind, above

60 right, left   gesture, signal   both, together

If the letters of the word BRIGHTEN are put into alphabetical order, which comes:

61 sixth? _____   **62** fourth? _____   **63** eighth? _____

GREEN   BLUE   BLACK   BROWN   GREY

If these colours are put in alphabetical order, which comes:

64 first? ________________   **65** fifth? ________________

At a summer camp, five children wore either blue, green or red shorts and either red, blue or green shirts.

Two children wore red shorts, two wore blue shorts and one wore green.

Two children wore green shirts, two wore blue shirts and one wore red.

John wore blue shorts and shirt. He was the only one to wear one colour.

Leena wore red shorts and Sam wore a blue shirt.

Sarah had one colour in common with Leena.

Micah wore green shorts.

From the information, work out which child wore which clothes and answer the questions.

66 What colour was Micah's shirt?________________

67 What was the colour Sarah had in common with Leena? ________________

68 Who wore the red shirt? ________________

69 Who, besides John, wore blue shorts? ________________

70 Who wore red shorts and a blue shirt? ________________

Find the two letters that will end the first word and start the second word.

Example pas (ta) ste

71 be (__ __) ch

72 sh (__ __) en

73 mu (__ __) ild

74 mi (__ __) ntre

75 sp (__ __) der

5

Underline the one word in the brackets which will go equally well with each of the words outside the brackets.

Example word, paragraph, sentence   (pen, cap, <u>letter</u>, top, stop)

76 feathers, fur, scales   (bird, lizard, cat, skin, fish)

77 comma, full stop, question mark   (sentence, page, speech, apostrophe, number)

78 metre, hectare, kilogram   (weight, height, length, mass, centimetre)

79 roll, loaf, bap   (cake, hot dog, bread, slice, cupcake)

80 steel, iron, tin   (can, metal, diamond, spoon, stainless)

5

Find a word that can be put either in front or at the end of each of the following words to make new, compound words.

Example cast   fall   ward   pour   <u>down</u>

81 grey   blood   fox   wolf   __________

82 jumping   ground   down   case   __________

83 burn   line   ways   step   __________

84 back   able   phone   roll   __________

85 chair   fire   post   sports   __________

5

Now go to the Progress Chart to record your score!   Total   85